The buzz about the Ask Anything J

"It's so cool that I don't have to ask my mom questions in person. She just writes back and I get an answer."

—DM, boy, 10, Seattle, WA

"The flip book bees are SO cute!"

—SG, girl, 9, Seattle, WA

"I hate asking my dad about this kind of stuff, so this makes it easier."

—TL, boy, 12, Bellevue, WA

"I had no idea my mom had such a huge crush on her best friend who was a boy when she was my age!"

—JK, girl, 11, Seattle, WA

"This journal is fun."

—SB, 8, Seattle, WA

"I wish I had something like this when I was a kid. I had so many questions and was too shy to ask my parents. My kids seem to really like this and I do too!"

—FT, mom to 9 and 11 year olds, Kirkland, WA

"I was nervous at first about the kinds of questions my kids would ask, but it's been really great. We get some "can I spend the night with so-and-so" type questions, but also lots of questions about puberty. What a great door opener."

—JG, mom to 8 and 10 year old girls, Seattle, WA

The

Ask ANYTHING Journal

Because an honest question deserves an honest answer.

Birds + Bees + Kids® LLC
birdsandbeesandkids.com
206-661-2245

Design, illustration and flipbook animation: Christine Marie Larsen / ChristineLarsen.com

ISBN: 978-1-59849-090-9

Printed in the USA

Peanut Butter Publishing
2925 Fairview Avenue East
Seattle, Washington 98102
877-728-8837
www.peanutbutterpublishing.com

Hey!

Parents know kids have questions about all sorts of things. They also know it's hard to just walk up and ask them about some stuff.

You might have questions about life, love, bodies, relationships, sex, drugs, friendships, spirituality, death and anything in between.

You can use this journal to ask your parents questions without having to stare them in the face.

By signing below, your parent(s) agree to answer any question you have as honestly as they can, to keep your questions private and to respect you and your opinions, even if they don't agree!

________________________ ________________________

Sometimes it might take your parents a while to answer your question, maybe because they need to figure out the answer. They may also want to keep some information private and decide not to answer your question. This might be annoying, but everyone has a right to privacy, including you.

Pass it back and forth from bed pillow to bed pillow or have a special spot in your room for the journal.

Remember – this journal belongs to ***you*** – so you decide how it's used.

Take care,

Amy G

Getting the buzz started!

Here are some questions you could ask your parent.

How do you know if you are in love?

Who was your first boyfriend/girlfriend?

Why can adults drink alcohol, but kids can't?

What is your first memory?

What's the smartest thing you've ever done?

What were you like as a kid? As a teenager?

What do you like the most about me?

If you could change one thing about yourself, what would it be?

When can I start dating?

What do you think happens when you die?

How will I know puberty has started?

How did you meet my mom/dad?

You get the idea – ask anything!

A quick note from your trustworthy question answerer!

Books

These books are all about reproduction and changing bodies. You can get them at the library, a bookstore or ask your parents to buy you some.

Recommended for ages 6 +

What's the Big Secret? Laurie Krasny Brown, Ed.D. and Mark Brown
It's SO Amazing! A book about eggs, sperm, birth, babies and families Robie Harris
Where Did I Come From? Peter Mayle
Your Body Belongs to You Cornelia Spelman and Teri Weidner

Recommended for ages 9 +

It's Perfectly Normal! Changing bodies, growing up, sex and sexual health Robie Harris
What's Happening to Me? Peter Mayle
The Care & Keeping of YOU: The body book for girls (American Girl Library) Valerie Schaefer
The Boy's Body Book: Everything you need to know for growing up YOU! Kelly Dunham and Steven Bjorkman

Recommended for ages 11 +

The "What's Happening to My Body?" Book for Girls Lynda Madaras with Area Madaras
What's Going on Down There? Answers to questions boys find hard to ask Karen Gravelle with Nick and Chava Castro
Changing Bodies – Changing Lives Ruth Bell and others
Body Drama – Real Girls, Real Bodies, Real Issues, Real Answers Nancy Redd

How do you know
if you are in love?

Who was your first boyfriend/girlfriend?

Why can adults drink alcohol, but kids can't?

What is your
first memory?

What's the smartest thing you've ever done?

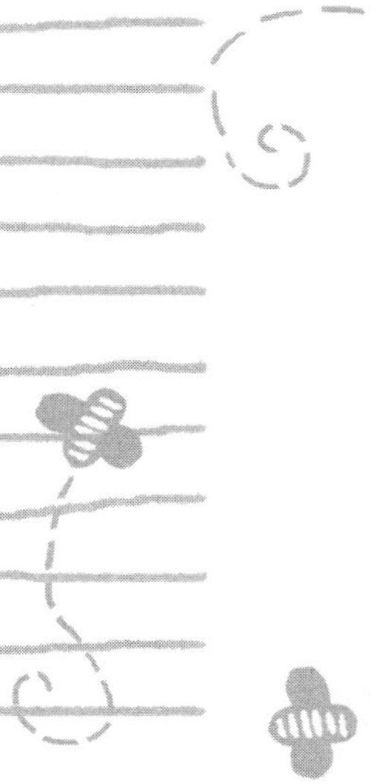

What were you like as a kid? As a teenager?

What do you like
the most about me?

If you could change one thing about yourself, what would it be?

When can I
start dating?

What do you think happens when you die?

How will I know
puberty has started?

How did you meet
my mom/dad?

In addition to teaching what to say and when, how to keep kids safe, and tips and tricks to make the conversations more effective, Amy Lang, MA provides parents and caregivers with an environment that encourages them to explore their personal values about sexuality, love, and relationships. Her goal is to help parents decide what is right for their family based on their values. She also works with professionals to help them learn about natural and healthy childhood sexual behaviors and when to be concerned. She lives in Seattle, has been married for over fifteen years and has a young son who keeps her on her toes playing Legos, digging and answering questions like, "How long do you have to lie like that?" when they talk about how babies are made. Amy is also the author of ***Birds + Bees + YOUR Kids - A guide to sharing your beliefs about sexuality, love, and relationships****.*